You're Very
SPECIAL
to Me

Douglas Pagels

Blue Mountain Arts ®
Boulder, Colorado

I want this book to put a smile on your face.

I want it to remind you that you have been on my mind. I want it to tell you that I think you're wonderful. I want it to be a beautiful part of this day.

Amo -
christmas 2009
deres to many
more christmas'
together
i like you
high fives!

To:

Kimo

From:

Kelly xo

ISBN: 0-88396-954-8

Certain trademarks are used under license.

Manufactured in China.
First Printing: 2005

This book is printed on recycled paper.

Blue Mountain Arts, Inc.
P.O. Box 4549, Boulder, Colorado 80306

And I want it to help you remember — every time you see it in the days to come — that this book was given to you just because…

you're *very special* to me.

Do You Know
How Important
You Are to Me?

☆☆

I hold you and your
happiness within my
heart each and
every day.

I am so grateful for
you, and so thankful to
the years that have
given me so much
to be thankful for.

I Care
So Much
About You

I care about you
more than I can say.
And that caring and
that feeling have a
meaning that is more
precious to me than
I can explain. But let
me try to tell you this…

Saying "I care" means that I will always do everything I can to understand. It means that you can trust me, that you can tell me what's wrong, that I will fix whatever I can, and that I will always be here for you.

You are a truly
special person.

Even if you were only
half as wonderful
as you are…

You'd still be twice
as nice as anyone
I've ever known.

It Takes a
Certain Kind
of Person
to Be Special

✰✩

It takes someone who is really wonderful; someone who lights up the world with feelings of friendship and love and understanding. It takes a truly unique personality and a knack for making life happier and more rewarding…

It takes someone who's
willing to take the time.
It takes an individual
who is able to open up
and share their
innermost feelings with
another. It takes
someone who makes the
path of life an easier
and more beautiful

journey. It takes a rare combination of many qualities interwoven with another person's life. It takes a certain kind of person to be special.

It takes someone
…exactly like you.

I Don't Know
What I'd Do
Without You

Sometimes we need
reminders in our lives
of how much people care.

If you ever get that
feeling, I want you to
remember this: Beyond
words that can even
begin to tell you
how much…

all my nicest memories.

When you hold this in
your hands, I want you
to think of me smiling
softly at you,
and thanking you…

for all that you are
  …to me.

I want to say that you are incredibly special to me. You are so important to my days and so essential to the smile within me. That space where our lives overlap is the place that brings me so much joy, understanding, and

The little book you hold in your hands is a very special book. Not just because it's from me… but because it says something I want you to know today — and that I want you to remember forever. Within the words on these pages…

To you:

For keeping my spirits up.
For never letting me down.
For being here for me.
For knowing I'm there for you…

For bringing so many
smiles my way.
For being sensitive to
my needs.
For knowing just what to say.
For listening better than
anyone else.

For bringing me laughter.
For bringing me light.

For understanding so much about me.
For trusting me with so much about you.

For being the best.
For being so beautiful.

I don't know what
I'd do… without you.

People like you are few
and far between. You
are the special kind
of person the world
needs more of.

People like you
make everything
so much nicer.

You have a marvelous
ability to turn
happiness into joy
and sadness into
understanding. You are
appreciated beyond
words, because people
like you mean the world
to… people like me.

Just a Little
Thought for
You to Keep

Though I can't always
be there with you, these
words can be. So I want
you to save this in a
special place and, every
now and then, think of
me. I want you to set
this aside and remember
it when you're feeling…

wonderful, so it can remind you: that's just how you make me feel. And save it for the days when the clouds are hanging around a little longer than they should, and maybe it will help to cheer you up.

When you get home in
the days to come and
see this little book
sitting on your dresser
or your shelf, remember
that I'm here, smiling
to myself, whenever
I think of all the
wonderful things…
about you.

You deserve to know
how special you are.
You… of all people…
should have the
privilege of knowing
how much nicer life is
with you in it.

And though those words
don't get shared as
often as I would like
them to, I would like
you to know — today
and always — that there
aren't many people in
this world who even
begin to compare
with you.

Thoughts
for You

☆☆

The Book
You Hold
in Your Hands

🍀

is exactly how I feel
about you.

You matter more to me
than you can imagine
and much more than
I'll ever be able
to explain.

One of the most special
places in my heart
will always be
saved for you.

You… the one person
I can always talk to;
the one person who
always understands…

You… for making me laugh in the rain, for helping me shoulder my troubles; for always putting me back on my feet again; and for giving me someone to believe in… someone who lets me know that

there really is goodness
and kindness and
laughter and love
in the world.

You… for being
one of the best
parts of my life,
and proving it over
and over again.

Everyone Needs Someone like You

Everyone needs someone
who is always there and
always caring. Everyone
needs someone who is
just a message or a
touch or a phone call
away; someone with whom
you can share everything
that's in your heart or
talk about the day in a…

special way that only
the two of you can.

Everyone needs someone
to encourage them; to
give a pat on the back
when things have gone
right, and a shoulder
to cry on when
they haven't.

Everyone needs someone
to remind them to keep
trying and that it will
all work out.

I hope
everyone
has someone
who's as wonderful
as you.

Would it surprise you
to know how many
wonderful thoughts
you are such
a special part of?

Well… there is one
thing I hope won't
surprise you
even a little bit:

It's that you are
absolutely cherished
by me. You
always will be.

And I'm so glad
that my world
has a blessing
as beautiful as you
in it.

If someone were
to ask me the secrets
of happiness
and gratitude
and serenity,
I know exactly
what I'd do…

I'd tell them to make
sure that they have
a person in
their lives
who's as precious,
as special, and
as wonderful as you.

I find myself thinking about you so much of the time… about how lucky I am to have you as a part of my days, what a good person you are, and about all the things you contribute to making my world a better place to be.

If it weren't for you,
I wouldn't have half
the happiness that I
feel inside.

I don't know what magic
it is that makes people
as wonderful as you…
but I'm sure glad
that it works.

Thoughts to Remember Forever

It seems like I'm always searching for a way to tell you how wonderful I think you are.

And I thought that maybe this book could help me convey a few thoughts that I would love to share with you…

You're my definition of a special person.

I think you're fantastic. And exceptional and unique and endearing. To me, you're someone who is very necessary to my well-being. In so many ways, you fill my

life with happiness and
the sweet feelings of
being so grateful and
appreciative that
you're here.
I could go on and on…
but you get the picture.

I think you're
a masterpiece.